Original title:
Breezes of the Tropics

Copyright © 2025 Creative Arts Management OÜ
All rights reserved.

Author: Gabriel Kingsley
ISBN HARDBACK: 978-1-80581-481-8
ISBN PAPERBACK: 978-1-80581-008-7
ISBN EBOOK: 978-1-80581-481-8

Celebration of the Soft and Gentle

Laughter floats on gentle air,
Palm fronds dance without a care,
Sun hats wobble on our heads,
As we dodge the coconut spreads.

Joyful shouts from every side,
While piña coladas slide,
We chase the ice cream truck around,
While flip-flops clack and bounce the ground.

Caress of the Coastal Tide

Waves tickle toes, it's quite a sight,
Seagulls dance, their flappy flight,
Sand castles made with silly pride,
Toppling down, oh what a slide!

Sand in our shorts, a grainy tale,
Shells and crabs— they set the scale,
As we squeal, a splash nearby,
In a sea of giggles, we forgot to dry.

Silhouettes in the Evening Glow

Sunset whispers, colors glow,
Shadow dancers in a row,
With lemonade we're feeling fine,
As fireflies join our silly line.

Laughter bubbles with the breeze,
As we try to catch our keys,
A clumsy jump and down we go,
In the soft light's playful show.

Nexus of Nature and Spirit

In the tree tops, monkeys tease,
While we sway with utmost ease,
Underneath a leafy dome,
Our laughter makes the jungle home.

Coconuts might drop and roll,
As we find our silly soul,
Nature's giggles fill the night,
In this joyful, wild delight.

Tranquil Veils of Dawn

Morning whispers play a prank,
Palm trees dance, their trunks in rank.
A parrot squawks a joke or two,
While all the roosters laugh and coo.

Sunlight slips like butter on toast,
A crab competes with the toast's boast.
The ocean giggles, waves on a roll,
As fish dive deep, enacting a stroll.

Respite in the Island Shelter

Hammocks swing with sleepy glee,
As monkeys play a game of spree.
With every sway, a coconut falls,
And someone yells, 'Watch out for those balls!'

Laughter bubbles like soda drinks,
While seagulls gossip and wink.
The sun takes a dip, it's a splashy scene,
As folks in flip-flops chase a jellybean.

Fermentation of Color and Sound

Paint the sky with guava juice,
While laughter grows like wild caboose.
The flowers sprout a melody bold,
With every note, a story unfolds.

Colorful fish join in the fun,
With fins that shimmer like the sun.
They sing a tune, oh what a sight,
While snorkelers play hide and seek at night.

Journey of the Wayward Wind

The wind plays tag with trees so tall,
Spinning hats upon a beach ball.
It teases waves to take a leap,
While sunbathers giggle, lost in sleep.

A kite takes flight, a daring feat,
As seagulls quarrel over a treat.
The wind whispers secrets, cheeky and bright,
As it tickles the cheeks of tourists in flight.

Fables Carried on Sweet Winds

A monkey found a hat one day,
He wore it sideways, felt so sway.
It flew off high, oh what a sight,
The parrot laughed, 'You look just right!'

The coconut dropped, a big surprise,
The monkey slipped, to his demise!
Yet up he got, with joyful grin,
'Next time I'll wear my shoes, not skin!'

Veils of Fragrant Air

The flowers danced with pollen cheer,
A bee buzzed past, oh dear, oh dear!
He tripped on petals, did a spin,
'Is this a party? Shall I dive in?'

The breeze grabbed scents of jasmine sweet,
Spreading laughter from head to feet.
The bee just smiled, and with a wink,
'Who knew that air could make us think!'

Secrets Hidden in the Wind's Embrace

A lizard lounged upon a stone,
'The wind's a prankster,' he had known.
It tickled tails, sent hats in flight,
'Catch me if you can!' said the light.

A chameleon turned to match the breeze,
'Who knows my color? Can't you see?'
With giggles echoed through the trees,
'This game of hide is such a tease!'

Conversations with the Sunlit Sky

The clouds were fluffy, white like cream,
A bird sat perched, in sunbeam's gleam.
'Can clouds get stuck? Oh what a plight!'
The sky just chuckled, 'Not tonight!'

A wishful wave, a dream from afar,
'Will we float high, like star to star?'
The sun replied, with a wink so sly,
'To shine is fun, just give it a try!'

Tides Turned by Gentle Winds

The palm trees dance with glee,
As if they've had too much tea.
Coconuts giggle in the air,
While flip-flops race without a care.

The sun's a jester, shining bright,
Daft seagulls squawk in sheer delight.
Sand castles wobble, then they fall,
As toddlers chase them, giggling all.

Notes of Honey and Haze

A lizard struts in shades of lime,
Winking at the world, full of rhyme.
Honey drips from frisky trees,
Sticky hands wave carefree in the breeze.

The hammock laughs with every swing,
As crickets chirp their silly bling.
Mangoes tumble, oh what a sight,
As squirrels applaud this fruity flight.

Conversation of the Seashells

Seashells gossip on the shore,
Trading tales of ocean lore.
"Did you see that crab's new dance?"
"Not as fab as my last romance!"

With snickers shared in salty air,
They whisper secrets without a care.
The tide rolls in with a sassy wave,
Reminding shells to be a bit brave.

Flickers of Stardust over Waves

The moon is winking, oh so bright,
As starfish giggle in the night.
Crabs host a party on the sand,
While fish flash lights with a band.

Whispers ripple through the tide,
As jellyfish glide with humorous pride.
"Catch me if you can!" they tease,
Leaving behind a trail of ease.

A Voyage in Whispering Currents

A little boat with sails so bright,
Drifting through the day and night.
The captain sneezes, oh what a sound,
Fish jump high, then flop around!

Coconut hats and laughter loud,
Sunburned cheeks form quite a crowd.
Seagulls giggle and steal our fries,
As we wave farewell to silly skies!

Essence of the Ocean's Sigh

The waves do dance, they twist and twirl,
While crabs in tuxedos make me hurl.
A jellyfish floats, lost in a daze,
Thinking it's part of a salsa craze!

Flippers worn, we jump and spin,
Chasing seahorses, what a win!
But watch your step, it's not so clear,
Sand castles topple, my dear, oh dear!

Petals on the Wind's Journey

Petals swirl in a cheeky dance,
Like toucans hoping for a chance.
The monkey swings, a playful sight,
Sipping juice with sheer delight!

A pineapple sings a tune so sweet,
As crickets leap on little feet.
"Hurry up," the hibiscus shouts,
"Frogs are late for our tree-top bouts!"

Tropical Ghosts in Silent Skies

There's a ghost with a palm leaf hat,
Swinging low, he's quite the brat.
He tickles toes and makes them squeal,
With coconut jokes, can you feel?

Laughter echoes through the night,
As lizards dance, oh what a sight!
They plot a prank on sleepy folks,
While parrots mimic the funniest jokes!

Lullabies from the Palms

In the coconut tree, a squirrel sings,
While my hat takes flight on invisible wings.
The parrots laugh, oh what a scene,
As I chase my shade like a playful Marine.

The lizards dance on a sunlit path,
While crabs play tag, it's a comical bath.
Oh, the warmth tickles everyone near,
As we wobble and giggle, fueled by good cheer.

Echoes of Sunlit Air

A gentle tug on my beachy attire,
As sand pelicans tease, like a mischievous choir.
The sun's bright smile, with a wink it plays,
While I lose my grip on a fruity daze.

Seashells gossip, nestled in a heap,
While I snore on the shore, in a sandy sleep.
The tides roll in, with a splash and a cheer,
And I wake up just in time for more beer.

Serenade of the Ocean's Breath

A crab with a drum, tapping out a tune,
As I trip on a flip-flop, under the moon.
The waves laugh and tumble, joyfully tossed,
While I write a note to my sanity lost.

Dancing with shadows, the palm fronds sway,
As a lizard sneaks by, in the sun's warm spray.
I'm caught between giggles and pretty seashells,
This paradise is where funny humor dwells.

Hues of Warmth in the Breeze

A bottle of lotion take flight in the air,
Chased by a seashell, oh what a rare affair!
The sun paints us funny, in colors so bright,
Wearing sunglasses at noon makes it a sight.

Bananas in hammocks, swinging with flair,
While my drink's a runaway, splashing everywhere.
The jellyfish wink, with a nod and a bounce,
And I laugh with the ocean, as I try to pounce.

Soft Kisses from the Coconut Trees

Coconuts giggle, swaying in glee,
Whispering secrets to the honeybee.
Palm leaves dance like a clumsy ballerina,
While monkeys plot pranks near a rusty marina.

Bananas await, ready to slip,
Launching a fruit on an unexpected trip.
Smiles erupt as a splash takes flight,
The island's laughter echoes, pure delight.

Tides of Air and Sunlit Waves

Waves surfacing with a zany trot,
Seagulls arguing over this and that spot.
They squawk like comedians in a play,
While sunbeams wink and join in the fray.

Flip-flops flopping on sandy shores,
A parrot mimics as he opens doors.
With every gust, a slip or a sway,
We laugh and tumble, come what may.

Embracing the Island's Exhale

A gentle puff sends a hat on a chase,
Spinning around like it's in a race.
Tanned tourists laugh as they chase the breeze,
Rolling on sand like a group of unease.

The palm trees chime with a rustling tune,
As beach balls bounce like they're dancing to June.
With each little gust, a silly parade,
The island's breath is hilariously played.

Wind-Swept Tales of Faraway Shores

The wind tells stories of fish at the bar,
Where mermaids sip juice and drive a car.
A crab does the cha-cha, all out of sync,
While laughter bubbles like a fizzy drink.

A flip-flop flies over a humorous scene,
With beachgoers dodging like they've seen a machine.
As laughter flows and the sun starts to set,
We forget our worries—this place is a net.

The Gentle Touch of Paradise

Palm trees sway like dancers low,
While coconuts drop in a lazy show.
Flip-flops flip, they stroll, they slide,
Even the sea crabs join the ride.

Sunburned tourists with sunglasses wide,
Complaining of sand that seems to abide.
Seagulls steal chips, oh what a crime,
In this tropical kingdom, we're losing time.

Melodies of the Coastal Whispers

The waves hum tunes of a jellyfish band,
Shrimp do the tango on the warm sand.
Surfboards tumble, they rearrange,
While sunscreen wars feel rather strange.

A fish jumps high, makes a splash so grand,
While sunbathers argue over tan plans.
Laughter echoes, the heat is rife,
Who knew the tide could have such a life?

Secret Paths of Wind and Sun

Kites are flying, caught in a dance,
Chasing the breeze like it's some romance.
A crab tries to race a toddler's toy,
While tourists search for the next free joy.

Birds pull pranks as they dive and swoop,
Joining the age-old beach ball troop.
In this warmth where silliness replays,
We embrace the sun in hilarious ways.

Driftwood Dreams on Gentle Currents

Driftwood floats like a log on a quest,
While beach buckets sit in their sand nest.
Entangled laughter, some sunburns too,
What's life without laughter beneath skies so blue?

Children giggle, chasing shadows they find,
While old folks nap, completely resigned.
In this paradise, where chuckles reside,
Fun's the main course, let joy be our guide.

Cauldron of Daydreams

In a pot of sunlit schemes,
Where the lizards play at dreams,
Coconuts wear tiny hats,
As the parrots crack up chats.

Sandcastles lean and sway,
While the crabs dance in dismay,
With flip-flops that take flight,
Making everyone take a bite.

Sipping fruit punch, very sweet,
A squirrel steals my tasty treat,
Umbrellas spin like crazy wheels,
While I crack up over my meals.

The golden sun starts to slide,
As jellyfish take on a ride,
With a giggle and a jest,
Tomorrow's more, I must confess!

Nightfall's Feathered Secrets

When the moon begins to glow,
Chickens try to steal the show,
Peacocks strut in twinkly shoes,
As the crickets sing their blues.

Under stars, a raccoon jokes,
Dancing with the clever folks,
A bat in shades, he flies so low,
As a walrus starts the show.

The palm trees whisper fleet,
Of the laughter on the street,
A parrot tells a funny tale,
Of a fish who learned to sail.

With each giggle, shadows creep,
As the sun is set for sleep,
Day will break, with happy schemes,
But tonight, we've got our dreams!

Threads of the Coconut Whisper

Coconuts gossip on the shore,
While sea turtles, they implore,
A crab with shades and a sit-up stance,
Can't help but lead a twilight dance.

Mangoes roll on sandy tracks,
While alligators play pranks,
With a toucan named Bob the Wise,
Chasing butterflies in disguise.

The sea breeze plays a playful tune,
As I toss a flip-flop to the moon,
And the hammocks wave in rhyme,
With dreams of pudding and lime.

With giggles bouncing all around,
The sandy shores are joy unbound,
Tomorrow's chill rests on our feet,
But tonight, oh what a treat!

Reluctant Farewells on Island Time

The sun waves goodbye, but it's late,
As the turtles gather and wait,
With a flip of a fin, they shout,
"Let's not leave yet, there's fun about!"

The palm trees shake, they know the score,
As the breeze tickles the ocean's floor,
A crab, with style, dons a bow,
While the sea sings a funky vow.

With piña coladas and laughter wide,
Time rolls slow, like a fun-filled tide,
But as the stars begin to pry,
The iguanas all wave goodbye.

Yet tomorrow brings another round,
For the joy of life knows no bound,
So we linger on, just one more flight,
As island nights dance in delight!

Revelations at the Water's Edge

By the shore, the seagulls squawk,
Crabs dance silly, what a shock.
Flip-flops flying, laughter loud,
Sunburned folks chuckling proud.

Shells and sun hats washed away,
Beach balls bouncing in the play.
With every splash, a giggle grows,
As sunburnt noses hit the toes.

Sandcastles leaning, waves in fright,
A toddler's tantrum, what a sight!
Seashells stuffed in pockets tight,
As flip-flop chases steal the night.

Salt and sunscreen, scents of fun,
With ice cream melting in the sun.
At the water's edge, life unfolds,
A symphony of laughter bold.

Whispers of the Warm Winds

Tropical whispers tease the ears,
As beach chairs sway, racked with cheers.
Coconuts roll with every breeze,
Island tales told with such ease.

A hammock sways between two trees,
While lizards sunbathe, live with ease.
With sunglasses askew, a grin's wide,
In this slice of paradise, we slide.

Mangoes dance on picnic plates,
While sunburned tourists share their fates.
With fruity drinks spilling like dreams,
We laugh 'til the coconut cream screams.

The wind's a trickster, sly and spry,
Sailing hats off with a playful sigh.
Under this sun, with goofy glee,
We discover mirth, wild and free.

Dance of the Island Zephyr

The palm trees twirl, a shaky waltz,
As beachwear flaps, it makes us pulse.
Laughter threads the salty air,
Where flip-flops stumble without care.

An old man danced, forgot his shoes,
Wearing just socks and a bright pink snooze.
As kids rush past in a high-speed chase,
The island wind brings a silly face.

With every breeze, the sunscreen flies,
Sticky and sweet, it meets our eyes.
As crabs walk sideways, eyes all aglow,
We join the parade, row by row.

Sunshine glitters, laughter sings,
In this wild tangle, joy springs.
With goofy steps on sandy floors,
We dance while our coconut's snore.

Caress of Tropical Currents

In the shallows, waves pull tight,
Splashing mishaps, oh what a sight!
Sandy toes and sunburned backs,
Join the tsunami of beachy quacks.

Ice cream treats begin to melt,
Sticky fingers, laughter dealt.
With every cold splash, giggles erupt,
In this tropical fun, we're fully corrupt.

A water balloon flung by mistake,
Lands on a sunbather, what a shake!
As everyone laughs, they flip and flop,
Pineapple hats might just make you stop.

The sea's our stage, a funny play,
With clumsy dives and summers' sway.
Each wave whispers of this delight,
In the sun-kissed bliss, we take flight.

Whispers of Palm Leaves

In the shade of palm trees, a secret's shared,
Monkeys giggle, swinging without a cared.
Coconuts tumble, a clumsy surprise,
Sipping pineapple juice while the seagull flies.

Everyone's dancing, even the crabs,
Doing the cha-cha, in funny jabs.
The breeze plays tricks, swaying the grass,
Watch out for flips, it's a riotous class.

A parrot squawks out a silly song,
While a turtle joins the cha-cha along.
Sun hats are flying, oh what a sight,
Who knew the tropics could be this bright!

As the sun sets and laughter glows,
In this tropical haven, joy surely flows.
The whispers of laughter, a curious sound,
With palmy mischief, we're all spellbound.

Dance of the Ocean's Caress

The waves curl up, they tickle the toes,
Crabs in tuxedos, oh how they pose!
Fish throw a party, oh what delight,
Jellyfish jiggle under moonlight bright.

Seashells collect stories in waves' embrace,
Starfish get dizzy, they pace and race.
Seagulls complain, the beach's too loud,
They flap and squawk, feeling quite proud.

A beach ball bounces, it flies to the sea,
Where dolphins perform, hamming with glee.
With every splash, the laughter ignites,
Ocean's own concert, under twinkling lights.

As evening falls, the waves still play,
In this zany dance, we lose our way.
With salty kisses and fun in the air,
The ocean's caress brings joy beyond compare.

Echoes of the Island Winds

The whispers of winds in the coconut trees,
Play tricks on the seas, they giggle with ease.
Kites in the sky, each one takes flight,
While the island winds whisper, "What a delight!"

A lizard wearing glasses, a true sea-fan,
Sings karaoke, the best in the land.
A breeze shakes the leaves, the laughter ignites,
"Hey! Who's that? Is it Uncle Sam's lights?"

Flip-flops are dancing, they groove on the sand,
Such hilarious movements, all perfectly planned.
Hammocks are swaying, cats take their chance,
To hop on the tides, and join in the dance.

As sunsets blaze, the island winds grin,
With chuckles and joy, let the fun begin.
In this carefree spirit, we all must abide,
Echoes of laughter, a thrilling ride.

Serenade of Sunlit Shores

The sun starts to shine, a glorious show,
On a beach full of laughter, where fun's in tow.
Flip-flops abandoned, the races begin,
Watch out for sandcastles gearing to win!

With sunburned noses, we sport silly hats,
Dancing with seagulls and giggling at cats.
Seashells keep secrets, tucked in their beds,
As the sun serenades with laughter that spreads.

A piñata of coconuts falls from the trees,
Candy rains down with a soft sizzling breeze.
Life's a big party in shades of sunshine,
Each smile and chuckle, oh, how they shine!

As day turns to evening, the moon takes its place,
With stories of joy and a playful embrace.
The shores hum a tune, in harmony's snare,
A serenade crafted with humor to share.

Spirits of Evening Mist

The night sneezed and the moon said, 'Bless!'
A parrot danced in a tiny dress.
Laughter spilled over like spilled drinks,
As fireflies buzzed and the palm tree winks.

With each step, the sand tickled feet,
While crabs clapped to a funky beat.
A coconut giggled, 'I'm not a nut!'
The stars shimmied, oh what a strut!

A lizard threw shade with a smirk so sly,
While a sunset painted the ocean high.
Fish told jokes in a splashy play,
Leaving the night with a smile on display.

So raise a toast to the quirks of the night,
Where the silly and wacky feel just right.
In this misty swirl where laughter insists,
Life's a grand circus, not one to resist!

Flutters of Exotic Fragrance

A wafting scent from a fruit we can't name,
Even a monkey expressed its disdain.
'Is that baked banana or rotten guava?'
As we giggled, our noses were in drama.

The flowers whispered with giggly grins,
Bees buzzed loudly, plotting their sins.
'No pollen for you!' shouted the sun,
As petals debated who would have fun.

A butterfly flapped in a tutu so bright,
While the breeze tangled its wings in delight.
The mango trees laughed as they swayed,
Playing hide and seek in the shade.

So let's twirl in this fragrant glee,
With all sorts of fruit on a bumblebee spree.
The laughter rises, let's dance a jig,
In this sweet-smelling world, oh how big!

Caress of Twilight Blues

In twilight's grip, a frog leaped high,
While the crickets chirped a lullaby.
The clouds wore pajamas, snug and blue,
As the stars said, 'Shall we start a zoo?'

A turtle told tales of daring quests,
While a cat gave side-eye, thinking it best.
'You're too slow,' chirped the quick-footed fly,
As the moon yawned, 'Oh my, oh my!'

Palm trees swayed in a stand-up show,
As a breeze tickled all in tow.
Waves whispered secrets to the sand,
While the sun waved goodbye, oh so grand.

So let's cozy up in a twilight hum,
With jokes and chuckles, we'll never be glum.
As the night unfolds and the silliness brews,
We'll laugh through the echoes of twilight blues.

Mosaic of Sound and Solitude

The night sighed softly, a kazoo went 'beep!',
While a seagull crooned us into sleep.
Heavy rhythms of the ocean's roar,
Danced with whispers from the palm-swayed floor.

A crab recited a nonsensical rhyme,
As a gecko checked its watch for prime time.
The coconuts giggled, 'It's party o'clock!'
While the waves played mirror to a jumping rock.

The rhythm of silence humbly crept,
As the stars watched on, cleverly inept.
With each note, the crickets made a fuss,
Throwing a concert just for us.

So let's join in this joyful refrain,
In this quirky, lovely, island domain.
With laughter and sounds we'll quietly weave,
Our own tune of joy and good cheer to achieve.

Soft Tides

When waves decide to wobble and dance,
They tickle feet, give sunbathers a chance.
With every splash, the laughter grows loud,
As seagulls dive down, all feeling proud.

Sandcastles crumble, but who really minds?
Each grain that falls is where joy unwinds.
The sun takes a dip, but not quite a soak,
Splashing in colors, with a bright tropical joke.

Gentle Rhythms

Palm trees sway as if telling a tale,
Of squirrels in shorts and a fellow withALE.
Tropical tunes blast from a shimmering dock,
As fishermen giggle, they reel in a rock!

With piña coladas in plastic coconuts,
They toast to good times and tease all the nuts.
The tide chimes in with a soft little grin,
As umbrellas dance, letting the fun begin.

Murmurs Beneath Coconut Trees

Coconuts chatter like old friends at noon,
While crabs do the cha-cha with a funky tune.
The breeze takes a bow, the sun gives a wink,
And the parrot squawks, while the island folks think.

Is that a ukulele or a honking seal?
The laughter flows freely, it spins like a wheel.
Under the palm shade, the secrets unfold,
As colorful stories of mischief are told.

Secrets of the Lagoon's Breath

Fish in bright colors gossip and play,
While the shrimp share their tales in an ocean ballet.
A turtle sings softly, with rhythm and rhyme,
Who knew that a lagoon could chill like fine wine?

In the shallows, the kids splash around,
Making chaos and bubbles, the laughter resounds.
The secrets they keep, are just pure delight,
As the sun sets their antics, it's quite a sight!

Swaying Shadows at Dusk

As the shadows stretch long, there's a fun parade,
With lizards in tuxedos and frogs serenade.
The stars peek through leaves with a wink of their eye,
While the crickets join in for a night-time sigh.

Dancing on beaches with flip-flops afloat,
The rhythm of laughter, the buoyant gloat.
Each footstep leaves footprints of giggles in sand,
In a quirky tropical wonderland, oh so grand!

Whispers of the Night Bloom

The moonlight dances on the ground,
While crickets play their silly sound.
A mango falls with a goofy thud,
And giggles echo from the mud.

The night sky wears a blanket of stars,
As lizards roam on tiny cars.
They'll race each other, with no care,
While fireflies joke about their glare.

Coconuts tell tales of their pride,
Of mermaids who take them for a ride.
The sea laughs hard, it's quite a show,
While parrots squawk, "Oh, don't be slow!"

Each gust of air is full of cheer,
Tickling noses, making them sneer.
With every pulse, the island sings,
As laughter floats on gentle wings.

Carried Away on Palm-Infused Air

Palm trees sway in a silly beat,
As monkeys dance with two left feet.
A breeze sweeps by, it tugs my hair,
And tells the ocean, "Have a dare!"

A crab performs a little jig,
While seagulls shout, "Oh, that's a big!"
The sand tickles toes, oh what a fright,
As shells pretend to take their flight.

In this warm blur of fun and glee,
Where every wave is a laughing spree.
Sunshine paints a grin on each face,
While shadows hide in a cozy space.

The air is thick with summer's glee,
With giggles floating wild and free.
So grab a drink, let worries sway,
In this playful paradise, we'll stay.

Glimpses of the Twilight Zephyr

At dusk, when colors play and swirl,
The world unveils a twinkling pearl.
A parrot jokes, "Where did I land?"
While lizards mimic an ice cream stand.

As twilight whispers to the sand,
A crab in shades takes a bold stand.
He struts around, so full of pride,
While children giggle, their mom's eyes wide.

The stars peek out, so shy and bright,
Pretending they're afraid of the night.
But the breeze shouts, "Come dance, don't hide!"
While seashells waltz, full of pride.

And as the day meets its funny end,
We gather close, our laughter to blend.
In this sweet moment, jokes take flight,
A memory made under the twilight.

Swaying Comfort of Island Nights

The hammock swings, a gentle ride,
As fireflies gather with delight.
They flash their lanterns, "Look at me!"
While sea turtles join the jubilee.

A coconut bobs on a merry stream,
Singing softly, "I'm living the dream!"
While crabs engage in a silly race,
With seaweed hats, they take their place.

The waves crack jokes, they splash and tease,
Whispering tales with the greatest ease.
Beneath the stars, the world feels right,
As laughter dances through the night.

So let's toast to this island fun,
Where every moment shines like the sun.
Join the choir of the joyful breeze,
And let our hearts sway with the trees.

Drift of the Quiet Tides

As the sea tickles my toes,
I giggle at fish in their clothes.
Jellyfish dance with a jolly sway,
Making the sharks think it's their play.

Seashells gossip, oh what a sound,
They whisper secrets all around.
The crabs in their snappy little suits,
Strut like they own the best of routes.

Palm trees sway with a cheeky grin,
While seagulls dive for their next win.
Who knew the ocean could be so wild?
It's a party where sea life beguiled!

Sunsets crash like a piñata blessed,
Filling the sky with colors dressed.
And I laugh as I watch them collide,
In this swirl of joy, I just glide.

Alignment of Waves and Whispers

The waves come in with a tickle and tease,
Making the beachgoers laugh with ease.
Whispers float like clouds on high,
While turtles join in, they just can't deny.

Sandcastles boast of their grand design,
Only to wash away with each brine.
Yet the builders just chuckle with cheer,
Creating new empires year after year.

Crabs wearing hats run a wild parade,
In this strange world, they aren't afraid.
They dance and clap with such delight,
Their tiny kingdom feels just right.

Seagulls drop snacks to the sand below,
Crafting a feast in this lively show.
Everyone munches, does a little jig,
As night falls down, they dance a big gig.

Kinship of Sunset and Sweet Breeze

The sun dips low with a playful wink,
While palm trees chatter, oh, let's not think.
Each gust of air is another grand jest,
Tumbling my drink, it loves to be blessed.

Waves whisper secrets with a splashy cheer,
While crabs rock out, they're no stranger here.
Birds trade jokes on the coconut high,
As they swoop low, claiming the sky.

Colors collide, a sky in a dance,
Pinks and oranges in a silly romance.
The laughter of nature fills the whole space,
As the sun bows out with a grin on its face.

And as the stars take their twinkling turn,
I chuckle at how these moments I yearn.
A world so funny, oh what a tease,
In the warmth of the night, I'm at ease.

Glorious Hues on the Horizon

Every sunset is a splash of delight,
Painting the clouds, a whimsical sight.
Splashing colors, oh what a thrill,
In this comedy show, I get my fill.

Gulls joke around, with snappy little dives,
While dolphins pop up, they're so full of jives.
Every flip is a giggle, every splash a grin,
In this vibrant canvas where fun begins.

Bright hues blend like a painter's dream,
As fishermen argue, "No, I'm supreme!"
Their nets get tangled, it's quite the show,
With laughter ringing, they each take a bow.

The night approaches, but who's in a race?
Stars giggle out loud, they love this place.
And as I leave, I know it's for good,
Till the next big laugh in this brotherhood.

Tangle of Vines and Air

In the jungle, laughter's found,
Vines are swinging all around.
A monkey slips, a parrot squawks,
While they trip on leafy stalks.

They swing and giggle, such a sight,
Bouncing off with all their might.
But tangled vines, oh what a tease,
Create a jungle game with ease!

Shadows of the Lush Understory

In shadows deep, where giggles bloom,
A sloth jokes, while finding room.
He takes a nap, what's the rush?
Dreams of eating, in a hush.

But here comes a wild raccoon thief,
He snickers softly, causing grief.
"What's in your pouch?" they all demand,
A stash of snacks, oh isn't he grand!

Whirl of the Hibiscus Dance

Petals spinning, what a ball!
Hummingbirds join in the thrall.
A flower giggles, coy and bright,
"Dance with me, let's take flight!"

From blooms to tips, they dip and dive,
With pollen laughing, oh they thrive!
But watch your head, here comes a bee,
"Oops, I'm sorry! Can't you see?"

Dreams on the Warm Breeze

The air is thick with sunny cheer,
A lizard grins, no hint of fear.
He slips on sunbeams, glints of gold,
With mischief twinkling, oh so bold.

A breeze whispers tales of the day,
While iguanas laugh and play.
Frogs croak jokes in a chorus tune,
And all feel happy 'neath the moon!

A Symphony of Colors in Motion

The parrot's squawk is quite the tune,
While the iguana poses by the moon.
A mango falls, rolls down the street,
Coconut hats make life so sweet.

Palm trees sway in a silly dance,
With every hip, a chance to prance.
Flip-flops flap in a merry beat,
Sunburned noses, can't take the heat!

Laughter spills with every wave,
Playing tag with a seagull brave.
Drinks with umbrellas, what a sight!
Cheers to fun from morn till night!

Tropical joy, under the sun,
Life here is far from being done.
In this vibrant splash, we stay afloat,
Join the fiesta, we're all remote!

Sands that Sing to a Soft Wind

The sand insists that it can talk,
In chicken scratch, it makes its guffaw.
Each grain a dancer, rattling free,
Spitting jokes like a jumping flea.

Footprints chase their own retreat,
A sneaky crab thinks it's so neat.
Sands that giggle under bare toes,
Ticklish tales that nobody knows.

Seagulls swoop with a cheeky grin,
Stealing snacks, they think they win.
Corn on the cob is their delight,
In this sandy theater, what a sight!

Sandcastles rise, then crash with flair,
Mighty turrets in midair share.
Build them up and watch them fall,
The laughter's worth it, after all!

Twilight's Caress on Coral Breezes

The sun dips down, it starts to glow,
While crickets hum a song so slow.
Evenings sparkle with firefly glee,
As stars don their little black spree.

Coral reefs giggle beneath the tide,
Fishes in bow ties take a ride.
Glowworms wink at shadows long,
Whispering secrets in the dark song.

Palm fronds flutter, telling tales,
Like children's laughter riding gales.
Every bumblebee brings its crew,
Buzzing along with a cocktail view.

Nighttime brings the party alive,
Dancing to the rhythm of the jive.
With every twinkle, we raise a cheer,
In this twilight, there's nothing to fear!

The Song of Solstice Winds

When the merry winds decide to play,
They twist and turn in a breezy ballet.
Mango trees sway with a burst of cheer,
As chilly cucumbers try to steer.

Dancers prancing on the sandy floor,
Flip-flops squeak as they roam and soar.
Palm trees shake hands with the lazy sun,
As tourists dive in just for fun.

Every breeze tells a yarn or two,
Of lost hats and a coconut stew.
Picnics tossed by a gusty tease,
What a ruckus among the trees!

So grab a laugh and hang around,
In the wind's wild tale, joy is found.
Raise your glass to the whims of fate,
With a wink and a grin, don't be late!

Lullabies from the Coral Cradle

In the cradle of waves, the fish start to dance,
A turtle in shades twirls, dreaming of France.
The seaweed sings softly, a lullaby bright,
While jellyfish giggle, glowing at night.

Crabs in tuxedos race under the sun,
Chasing their shadows, oh, what silly fun!
A clam with a shell that whistles and yawns,
Keeps time with a dolphin, who still wears his brawns.

While sharks play the banjo with tunes, oh so sweet,
The porpoises cheer, tapping their feet.
As bubbles of laughter, like pearls, do arise,
In this tuneful ocean, it's joy in disguise.

So, rest now, dear child, while the corals hum low,
For dreams filled with giggles will surely still flow.

Breath of the Mango Grove

In a grove full of mangos, the squirrels have flair,
Performing trapeze acts in mid-air with a stare.
The parrots tell jokes, while the monkeys just swing,
A pineapple hat is the latest in bling.

The mangoes all giggle, ripe with delight,
As the sun does a jig, oh, what a fine sight!
With each gust of warmth, laughter flies past,
The fruits and the critters are having a blast.

A lizard on stilts winks and struts by,
While worms in tuxedos all wave, oh so spry.
The breeze carries whispers of fruity banter,
As the nectar is sipped by a cheeky new canter.

So feast on the laughter, let the good times roll,
In the mango grove's heart, there's joy for the soul.

Melody of the Seagrape Canopy

Under seagrape leaves, the shadows do play,
The crickets compose tunes till the end of the day.
With waves as their chorus, they dance wild and free,
As a squirrel in shades shares his wisdom with glee.

A raccoon in a bowtie sips coconut milk,
While a seagull in pearls struts, as smooth as silk.
The rustle of leaves brings a chuckle or two,
As fireflies sparkle in their evening debut.

The breeze carries whispers, of jokes we all know,
Like why did the crab not share his fine dough?
Because he was shellfish, the punchline is clear,
While the moon grins on softly, lending a cheer.

So gather around, let the tales intertwine,
In the melody sweet, where laughter will shine.

Touch of the Warmth

With the sun on my face and a smile on my lips,
I dance with the shadows, do backflips and flips.
The warmth in the air tickles toes as I prance,
An island of giggles, oh, come join the dance!

A crab in a sunhat is sipping his tea,
While lizards play leapfrog, as happy as can be.
The breeze through the palms hums a whimsical tune,
And the days feel like magic from morning to moon.

With each little ripple, creations unfold,
Like fish in a talent show, brave and bold.
The warmth of their smiles, a contagious delight,
As the sassy old toucan jokes into the night.

So let laughter flutter like butterflies do,
In this land of the sunny, where joy feels brand new.

The Call of the Siren's Wind

With a whistle and a shout,
The parrots twist about,
They steal our fruity drinks,
And leave us with our winks.

A coconut hits Bob's head,
He laughs, then claims his bed,
Sandy toes and sunburned backs,
All forgotten in laughter's tracks.

The waves dance to a silly tune,
While crabs jive under the moon,
Siren songs of fun and cheer,
Pull us closer, never fear.

So let's toast with mango bliss,
Swaying in our sandy kiss,
As the wind continues to tease,
In this laughter-filled breeze.

Veils of the Sultry Afternoon

The sun hangs low in the sky,
As lizards wink and try,
To charm the ladies by the sand,
With their lizardy, awkward brand.

With a laugh, a drink spills wide,
It's not just fish that glide,
Our sunscreen winds up in the drink,
We giggle, barely able to think.

Palm fronds flap like hands in jest,
As we lounge without a quest,
Coconut shells filled with glee,
Look, there goes another bee!

We dance in shadows, spin and sway,
Chasing all our cares away,
The afternoon's quite the show,
In this warm wild wind we know.

Laughter of the Ocean Spray

The waves crash with a splish and splosh,
As seagulls cackle, flap and nosh,
Fish jump high, they make a splash,
We laugh till bellies jiggle and dash.

A toddler yells, 'Watch me dive!'
While dodging waves, he feels alive,
The ocean's tickle makes him squeal,
A slippery, fun-filled reel!

Shells scattered, treasure awaits,
We craft our crowns, it's our fate,
But watch for crabs, they're on the prowl,
They pinch our toes and make us howl!

The spray tickles like a friendly tease,
While we roll and giggle in the ease,
As laughter sings across the bay,
Every splash a joyful relay.

Petals in the Wind's Embrace

In the garden, a fluttering sight,
Dancing petals put up a fight,
They play tag with the passing breeze,
Sprinkling charm with perfect ease.

A parakeet, bright and bold,
Steals the show, or so I'm told,
As flowers bow to its arrival,
Each petal sways in survival.

We chase butterflies on a whim,
With twirling skirts, and laughter's hymn,
Stumbling as we try to catch,
These colorful dreams, a perfect match.

As laughter fills the fragrant air,
We hide from bees, but not a care,
In this floral jest, we find our place,
With petals dancing in sheer grace.

Hideaway of the Wind Chime

In a garden where the chimes complain,
The cats mistake them for some odd game.
They pounce and tumble, all in delight,
While the wind just giggles, taking flight.

A parrot squawks, a loud tune breaks,
The neighbors wonder what it takes.
To keep the laughter flowing so bright,
Amid swinging sounds that dance through the night.

Old ladies sway with teacups in hand,
They gossip and laugh like a jazzy band.
The muffins shake like maracas unplanned,
As breezy echoes tickle the land.

Under the moon where the shadows play,
We pop the corks as we sway.
The wind chime giggles, the night's in tune,
With silly secrets shared with the moon.

Shimmering Paths of the Evening Gale

The evening whispers with shimmery sass,
As the stars join in, all dressed up in glass.
We chase fireflies, with giggles galore,
Forget the map, who needs to explore?

A dog in shades struts down the street,
His tail wagging to a jazzy beat.
The breeze enthusiastically tries to woo,
Trouble is, it tangles the hair on you!

With kite in hand, I launch to the skies,
The wind just laughs, it's no surprise.
It flips and tumbles my joy in the air,
As I flail around without a care.

Oh, the dance of gusts, with shimmy and sway,
Everyone knows it's a silly ballet.
The evening gale whispers delightful spells,
Of laughter and joy, oh how it compels!

Portrait of the Setting Sun

A canvas painted in shades of surprise,
Where orange and pink play peek-a-boo skies.
The sun winks cheekily, drops to the floor,
While crickets prepare for their nightly encore.

Children giggle while chasing their dreams,
The sunset lingers, bursting at the seams.
With each splash of color, they clap and cheer,
The sky's a big show and all are near!

Silly shadows stretch, doing the splits,
As evening whispers all of its bits.
The clouds turn cotton candy in flight,
Painting this portrait with laughter so bright.

As day takes a bow and stars start to hum,
We leave our worries; just listen, here it comes!
The night wraps us tight in cozy delight,
Where giggles and dreams dance into the night.

Woven Threads of Sea and Sky

A splash of laughter where sea meets blue,
Seagulls chortle, it's all fun and view.
The waves wiggle, making silly faces,
As we dance on shores, exploring their spaces.

Kites fly high with a whoosh and a whirl,
Tangled up, making a dancer's twirl.
The kids laugh, trying to put them in line,
While I fall over, sipping my brine.

The horizon giggles, painted in glee,
While fish tease me, darting with glee.
I swear they wave as they swim on by,
Luring me closer, oh, don't be shy!

With oceans of joy and skies full of spin,
We weave through the laughter, let the fun begin.
And even the jellyfish join in the play,
Waving their bells, in a jelly-like way!

Interlude in a Moonlit Garden

In the garden, shadows dance,
With the laughter, plants prance.
A squirrel wearing a tiny hat,
Winks at flowers, oh how they chat.

Cucumbers giggle, tomatoes roll,
While radishes sing, they're on a stroll.
The moon's a disco ball, shining bright,
In this garden, all feels just right.

Crickets drumming with a beat,
Beetles try to tap their feet.
While the flowers share their jokes,
It's a comedy of clumsy folks.

And in this night of silly cheer,
Every leaf offers a pint of beer.
So join the fun, don't be a bore,
In this moonlit garden, forevermore.

Currents of Forgotten Dreams

In a stream of giggles and sighs,
Float the ducks in their funny ties.
They quack and splash without a care,
While frogs declare, 'We're debonair!'

Bubbles rise like bubbles of thought,
Making waves with laughs that are caught.
A turtle in shades takes a cruise,
Munching on doughnuts, singing the blues.

Fish gossip with glittery scales,
While a snail tells tales of the trails.
'With every flip, there's a chance to slip,'
Says a fish as it takes a dip.

These currents bring laughter anew,
As past dreams swirl, with a laugh or two.
In the muck, joy finds its way,
In this river, we'll forever stay.

Fusion of Light and Lushness

In a jungle sprouting giggles and spite,
Parrots wear shades, what a sight!
They squawk out jokes, loud and clear,
While monkeys swing, spreading good cheer.

Vines twist and twirl like they're in a dance,
Frogs leap, arguing about their chance.
With every rustle, a burst of glee,
'This vine is mine!' they shout, 'Can't you see?'

Sunbeams tickle the leaves up high,
As sloths slowly ponder how to fly.
'Yo, mate! It's just a matter of time,'
Sways the palm tree, spitting out rhymes.

In this lush realm of fun and light,
Every creature joins in the night.
So grab your friends, don't be shy,
Let's laugh till the sun says goodbye!

Ink of the Setting Sun

As the sky spills colors, laughter abounds,
Crabs in bow ties, playing around.
With the waves they dance and glide,
While seagulls cheer from the tide.

The horizon wears a golden crown,
As clumsy dolphins tumble down.
'This ink is thick with stories untold,'
Cries a clam, not quite bold.

Breezes whisper silly lore,
Jellyfish juggle, begging for more.
A sunset gala, all a charade,
With the tide pulling, mischief displayed.

So raise a glass to this day's end,
With every wave, laughter we send.
In colors bright, let's soak and run,
For this canvas is painted with fun!

Hushed Rustle of Tropical Night

The leaves giggle softly, swaying,
As crickets hold a concert, playing.
A lizard sneezes, it's quite absurd,
While frogs croon softly, how very absurd!

Stars twinkle like eyes, watching the show,
As palm trees dance, revel in the glow.
Insects mumble secrets, tickling the ear,
While the moon, in laughter, hovers near.

A coconut drops, with a thud so loud,
The monkeys laugh, oh, they're so proud!
A playful breeze teases the hammock low,
Swinging sleepy heads, then off they go.

So join the night in this silly spree,
Where every moment's as fun as can be.
In the hush of night, the laughter grows,
Amidst the rustle, anything goes!

Embrace of the Warm Air

The warmth wraps around like a comfy old chair,
As I fan myself with a slice of raw pear.
Fruits fall from trees, with a plop and a splash,
While birds dance nearby in a colorful flash.

Sweaty folks lounge with sun hats on heads,
While ice cream melts and dribbles, oh dread!
Kids chase after beach balls, bouncing and squeal,
As the sun plays peekaboo, a golden reel.

Coconuts wobble like they're in a race,
While sunburned tourists search for a place.
They stumble on sand and laugh at their plight,
Embracing the warmth, 'til day turns to night.

Here in this haven, all troubles take flight,
With a giggle here and a sun-soaked delight.
Embrace all the fun that the warm air brings,
With laughter and joy, oh, how the heart sings!

Currents of a Sun-Kissed Paradise

Waves giggle as they tickle the shore,
While flip-flops dance in the sand, what a score!
Seagulls squawk jokes, giving it their flair,
As kids splash in puddles without a care.

Ice-cold drinks clink, a fruity delight,
With umbrellas so silly, they're quite the sight.
A crab in a tux struts to the beat,
While tourists are wrestling, who's got the heat?

Surfboards tumble in a comical way,
As sunburns and laughter define the day.
Beach towels fly as the wind plays along,
Join the fun, where everything feels wrong!

In this sun-kissed paradise, joy abounds,
With giggles erupting in silly sounds.
So ride the waves of laughter and play,
And let the currents carry worries away.

Songs of the Verdant Hues

In the jungle of giggles, the leaves are alive,
With monkeys that chatter and brightly contrive.
A parrot squawks jokes, colorful and bold,
And lizards perform, a sight to behold.

Glorious colors blend in the fun,
While flowers shake hands with the gleaming sun.
Butterflies flit, they're putting on airs,
While ants choreograph, an army that dares.

Coconuts tumble, oh what a surprise,
And vines sing along with a whimsical rise.
The breeze tells tales of laughter and cheer,
Inviting all creatures to dance and not fear.

So let us enjoy the songs that we find,
In the verdant hues, where humor's entwined.
A world of vibrance, vivid and bright,
Where the symphony plays through day and night!

Rhapsody of Shimmering Waters

A fish in a hat, quite a sight,
Dancing in waves, morning light.
He wiggles and jigs, what a tease,
While seagulls complain, just with ease.

A coconut rolls, trying to run,
It slips on a wave, oh what fun!
A crab joins the dance, quick and spry,
Winks with a claw, oh my, oh my!

A sunken boat with a parrot squawks,
Rehearsing his lines as he mocks.
A beach ball goes sailing, round and round,
With antics galore and laughter abound.

What a show, with the sand as the stage,
Nature's own circus, it's all the rage.
So come on down to the splash and the tease,
Where everyday life is a playful breeze!

Echoing Lull

A hollow shell sings a silly tune,
While crabs do the cha-cha under the moon.
The waves clap their hands, oh what a sight,
In the chorus of night, everything feels right.

A lazy dog snores on the golden sand,
Dreaming of tennis balls, isn't it grand?
Laughter bubbles up from a nearby cart,
As a kid tries to juggle, bless his heart!

Stars peek above with a wink and a grin,
As the ocean whispers a soft, gentle spin.
The night tickles toes splashing near,
As laughter echoes, it's all we hold dear.

Twinkling lights dance on the water's face,
Each wave bringing joy, a warm embrace.
So come join the fun, let worries drift,
In nature's embrace, feel the day's gift!

Whispering Dawn

The sun yawns wide, stretching in gold,
While birds wear outfits, a sight to behold.
A rooster does cartwheels, what a display,
While sleepy heads shout, "Please, go away!"

Pineapples giggle from their sun-kissed trees,
Telling tall tales in the soft morning breeze.
A monkey unwraps a present of fruit,
Dancing around in a silly pursuit.

The ocean wakes up with a frothy roar,
As surfboards ride in, begging for more.
A crab with sunglasses, so cool and so sly,
Looks straight at you, with a wink of an eye.

What a delightful morning, so bright and new,
With laughter and fun, there's much to pursue.
Join the party, let your spirit soar,
In the playful dawn, there's laughter in store!

Intimacy of Stars and Surf

The stars tell secrets to the waves so bold,
While giggles and splashes are breaking the mold.
The moon wears a hat, quite stylish and neat,
Dancing on the water, oh, what a feat!

A surfboard floats by with a gal on a ride,
She waves to a crab, who's just filled with pride.
"A starfish can dance! Watch me twirl!" he shouts,
While tourists all cheer, disguising their doubts.

Palm trees sway gently, waving their arms,
As they share all the juicy and fanciful charms.
A shell starts to sing, oh, what a voice,
In the warm tropical air, it's the best choice.

So gather around, let's join in the fun,
With stars in the sky and the surf that has won.
In this whimsical place, where laughter can flow,
Let joy be the dance and let happiness glow!

Gift of the Tropical Sun

Bright rays of laughter shine down to play,
As giggling shells roll in the bright sun's ray.
A pineapple tumbles, sipping some tea,
While coconuts giggle, as happy as can be!

The sun wears sunglasses, oh what a flair,
While flip-flops race down without a care.
A squawking parrot tries knitting a net,
Weaving tales of adventure; what a safe bet!

At high noon the fun truly begins,
As jellyfish boogie with jellyfish grins.
A beach ball dances on the sand with glee,
While children build castles beside a palm tree.

So come take a dive into sunshine so bright,
With laughter and joy in the warm, golden light.
In this joyous playground, there's no place like home,
So let's celebrate life under sun's vibrant dome!

www.ingramcontent.com/pod-product-compliance
Lightning Source LLC
Chambersburg PA
CBHW072216070526
44585CB00015B/1369